Happy Diwali

Written by Claire Llewellyn

It is the first day
of Diwali.

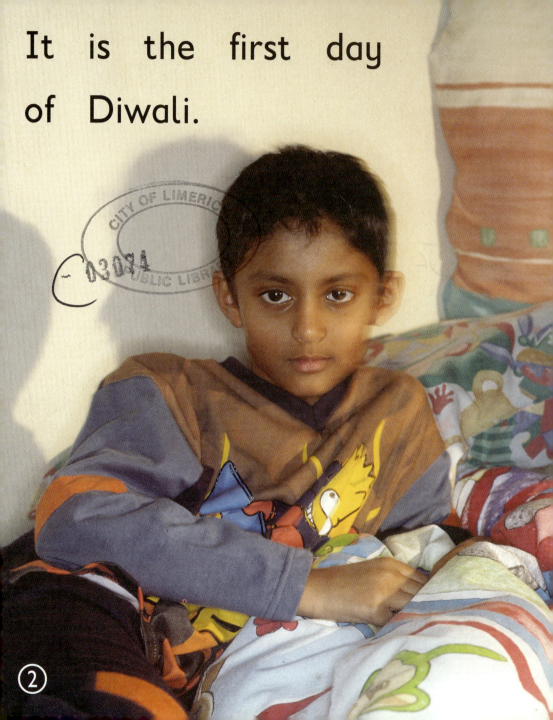

③

It is time to dress.

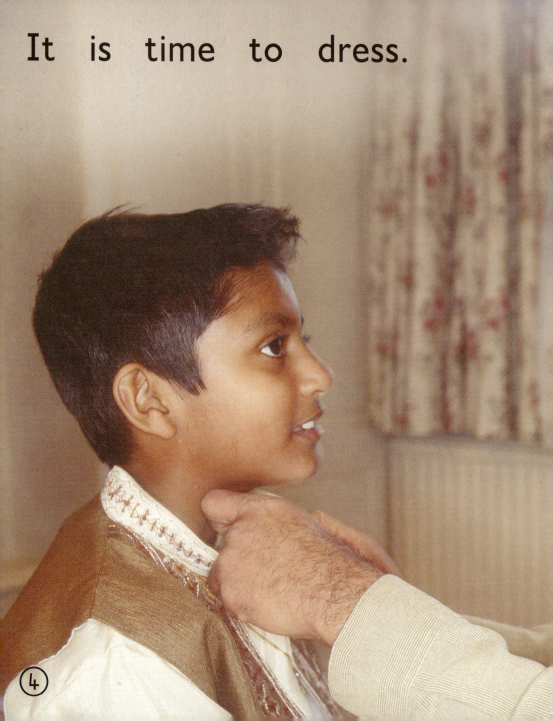

⑤

It is time to pray.

It is time for the presents.

It is time for the candles.

It is time for the food.

⑬

It is time for the fireworks!

⑮

Glossary

candle

dress

fireworks

food

pray

presents